W9-BRR-595

HAMPTON COURT PALACE

FRONT COVER and ABOVE: *The West Front showing the Great Gatehouse and the Bridge flanked by heraldic beasts.* FACING PAGE: (1) *Henry VIII who took possession of Wolsey's Palace.* (2) *Anne Boleyn, Henry's second wife. She gave her name to the famous gateway.* (3) *Jane Seymour, Henry's third queen. She died at Hampton Court after giving the king the son he so desperately wanted.* (4) *Catherine Howard, the fifth wife of Henry and second to die on the block. Her ghost is said to walk the Haunted Gallery.* (5) *Charles II who laid out the Home Park.* (6) *Sir Christopher Wren, architect of the State Apartments.* (7) *William III and* (8) *Mary II, joint sovereigns who "took great delight" in Hampton Court.* (9) *Queen Anne who added greatly to its splendour. Cardinal Wolsey, the builder, is seen on p. 4.*

HAMPTON COURT PALACE

Olwen Hedley

ALTHOUGH Hampton Court Palace was planned from the first on a regal scale, it was not originally a royal residence. It was built by Thomas Wolsey, "the proudest prelate that ever breathed", and presented by him to his master, King Henry VIII. The furnishings, tapestries and plate with which he had filled its rooms were included in the gift, which appears to have been made in 1525, when Wolsey already foresaw the decline of his power and the need to try to retain the king's favour.

He continued to enjoy the mansion as his own until his disgrace became imminent four years later. On 3 July 1529 he left Hampton Court, never to return. On 30 October his lands were declared forfeit to the king, who also claimed York House, Wolsey's London home as Archbishop of York. Renamed Whitehall, it continued to be the capital seat of the sovereign until it was accidentally burned down in 1698.

Even before Wolsey's death on 29 November 1530 the king had begun to enlarge Hampton Court, which was designed around the conventional sequence of courtyards. Wolsey's Great Gatehouse led from Outer Green Court on the west into Base Court, and this in turn to what is now called Clock Court, where the cardinal had his state and private apartments. Within six years King Henry had replaced the cardinal's great hall with

*   *   *

the one which stands today on the north side of Clock Court. At the east end of the palace he added Cloister Green Court, which was enclosed by a new lodging for himself on the south, a lodging for the queen adjacent to it on the east and Wolsey's chapel and long gallery on the north.

The Tudor royal apartments were demolished by Sir Christopher Wren, who built for King William III and Queen Mary II the State Apartments and private rooms which are so superb a feature of the palace today. Hampton Court is chiefly a memorial of its founder, Cardinal Wolsey, and the three sovereigns whose taste it most conspicuously displays, Henry VIII and William and Mary.

The history of the manor can be traced from 1086, when "Hamntone in the county of Middlesex" was described in Domesday Book. By the middle of the thirteenth century it was in the possession of the Knights Hospitallers of St. John of Jerusalem, who built a small manor-house on the site of the present palace. The retreat was not unknown to royalty. In 1338 extra expenses were allowed for guests

Continued on page 6

FACING PAGE (above): *The Great Gatehouse seen from Base Court, and (below) Anne Boleyn's Gateway leading eastward from Base Court into Clock Court. The latter is flanked by towers decorated by Giovanni da Maiano's roundels. Beyond the gateway on the left is the west end of the Great Hall.*

RIGHT: *The Astronomical Clock on the inner front of Anne Boleyn's Gateway is surmounted by a bell turret.*

3

FACING PAGE (above): *Wolsey's Closet. The early 16th-century paintings, which were done either for Wolsey or for Henry VIII, illustrate scenes from the Passion of Our Lord. The ornate gilt* gesso *ceiling bears Tudor roses and the feathers of the Prince of Wales. Below the frieze Wolsey's motto* Dominus michi adjutor *("The Lord my helper") appears again and again.* (Below): *The* Great Kitchen, *and Cardinal Wolsey who began to build Hampton Court for himself in 1514 and surrendered it to Henry VIII in 1529.*
ABOVE: *The Chapel Royal.*

"because the Duke of Cornwall lives near at hand". This was King Edward III's eldest son, later known as the Black Prince, to whom his father had given the palace of Sheen downstream on the Surrey side of the Thames. When King Henry VII rebuilt Sheen, calling it Richmond, he used Hampton Court as a retreat. Early in January 1503 his queen, Elizabeth of York, was rowed from one to the other in "a grete bote" with twelve rowers. She spent a week at Hampton Court praying for a safe confinement, but when a princess was born in February at the Tower of London both mother and child died.

King Henry VIII, the son of King Henry VII and Queen Elizabeth, himself visited Hampton Court on 20 March 1514, accompanied by his first consort, Catherine of Aragon. Wolsey, who was to become Archbishop of York that autumn, and a

cardinal and lord chancellor in the following year, had already fixed on the manor as his country residence. On 24 June 1514 he acquired it on lease from the Knights Hospitallers. A local legend says that before making his choice he employed "the most eminent physicians in England, and even called in the aid of doctors from Padua, to select the most healthy spot within twenty miles of London". All agreed to recommend Hampton Court on account of its "extraordinary salubrity".

While his palace was being built Wolsey enclosed the estate, which covers nearly 1800 acres, to form Hampton Court and Bushy Parks. In 1515 he was laying out gardens under his windows on the south front. His arbours and alleys "so pleasant and so dulce, The pestylent ayers with flavors to repulse", led to the river, like the walled Pond Garden today. When the

weather was inclement he took his evening recreation in the long gallery, an amenity favoured by him and quickly copied in other great houses. Like the other principal rooms, it was on the first floor.

Hampton Court already contained about 1000 rooms, all of which were used. The cardinal's own household numbered nearly 500 people, and there were always 280 silken beds available for visitors. When he received a distinguished French embassy in 1527 the guest chambers around

*   *   *

ABOVE: *The East Front. Four noble Corinthian pillars with a pediment above frame the windows of the Queen's Drawing Room.*

FACING PAGE: *The South Front has a simple centre-piece bearing the Latin inscription for "Built by William and Mary".*

Base Court "had hangings of wonderful value, and every place did glitter with innumerable vessels of gold and silver".

"Wolsey's Closet", a dazzlingly beautiful little room in the range east of Clock Court, is now the sole remnant of his personal apartments, which were enriched with moulded ceilings, coloured glass in the mullioned windows and arras of gold and silk on the oak-panelled walls. "One has to traverse eight rooms", reported the Venetian ambassador, "before one reaches his audience chamber, and they are all hung with tapestry, which is changed once a week". Like King Henry VIII, Wolsey was a discriminating collector and employed agents to procure the choicest examples from the looms of Flanders. Carpets added distinction to the state and private rooms. A gift of 60 reached the cardinal from Venice in 1521.

With exceptional refinement he also made his home a model of hygiene. Every part of Hampton Court was drained and rain water and refuse were carried by great brick sewers into the Thames. So sound was the system that it lasted until 1871. Nor did the palace lack an incoming supply of the purest water available. It came from the springs at Coombe Hill three miles away on the other side of the Thames, under which it was conveyed in leaden pipes. Hampton Court continued to receive water by this means until 1876 and the course of Wolsey's water-works can still be traced on the Ordnance Survey map. The palace was well provided with jakes, or water-closets, all the principal apartments having private ones.

Baths provided another agreeable feature. They appear to have been built by King Henry, as workmen were busy on the "baynes" in 1529-30

after he had taken possession of Hampton Court and begun to enlarge the palace. One of his first cares was to affix the tokens of royal ownership. Prominently displayed were "thre sondry tables of fre ston" carved by Edmund More, of Kingston, with "certen of the Kynges best [beasts, or supporters] holding up in a shilde the Kynges armes". These were placed on the outer and inner sides of the Great Gatehouse and on the front of the gatehouse leading from Base Court to Clock Court, where modern copies can now be seen.

Wolsey had already embellished the inner front of the second gatehouse, overlooking Clock Court, with his own arms in terracotta affixed to an archiepiscopal cross, supported by *putti* and surmounted by a cardinal's hat, with his motto, *Dominus michi adjutor,* below. The arms and hat were defaced by King Henry, but have been

Continued on page 10

FACING PAGE (above): *The colourful array of the Pond Garden, laid out c. 1700 and remodelled earlier this century.* At the end Wren's South Front joins Wolsey's buildings. On the left is the Lower Orangery. (Below): *The East* Front from the Great Fountain Garden. ABOVE: *The Great Hall where the king dined on a dais.*

skilfully restored. The panel was the work of an Italian artist, like the medallions of Roman emperors in terracotta on the flanking turrets of the gatehouse. Eight of these medallions were made for Hampton Court in 1521 by Giovanni da Maiano, who later provided a similar series to decorate the Holbein Gate at Whitehall. After the destruction of the Holbein Gate in 1759 two of the royal roundels found their way to Hampton Court, where today a total of ten can be counted on various gatehouses. They were originally coloured and gilded.

Although the second gatehouse bears so conspicuous a memorial of Wolsey, it has long been called Anne Boleyn's Gateway. The fan-vaulted ceiling, added after Anne became queen in 1533 and now restored, bears her personal badge, the falcon, and the intertwined initials H and A. During her reign, which ended with her execution on 19 May 1536, the Great Hall was completed and here too were erected symbols of her brief supremacy. Hers are the arms impaled with the royal arms among the foliage on the main supports of the hammer-beam roof, that wondrous structure which displays Italian influence although it was wrought by Englishmen. The gorgeous pendant lanterns were

carved by Richard Rydge of London, who received £3.3.4 for each of the "pendauntes standyng under the hammer beam" and £1.5.0 apiece for those in the arches above.

Rydge also carved four "pendenttes" around the opening into the louver, the smoke-vent high above the stone hearth in the middle of the floor, near the dais. The louver, now gone, was an elaborate hexagonal structure of three storeys, surrounded by four lions, four dragons and four greyhounds, each carrying a painted and gilded vane, with a great crowned lion on top holding "the great pryncipall vane baryng the close crowne". These were the loftiest of a host of vanes displaying the arms of King Henry and Anne Boleyn, which flashed and glittered, not only around the roof of the hall, but also from the lead cupolas on the turrets of the Great Gatehouse, then two storeys higher than it is today.

Although Anne Boleyn's arms and badge survived in the Great Hall and inner gatehouse, elsewhere they were replaced immediately after her death by those of the king's third wife, Jane Seymour, her former lady in waiting. The golden vanes were "payntyd and new alteryd from Quene Annes armes unto Queen Janes", and in the queen's

new lodging workmen hastily superimposed the initials JS over the discredited AB. The apartments were completed for Queen Jane and it was there that on 12 October 1537, St. Edward's Eve, she gave birth to the future King Edward VI. He was baptized three days later in Wolsey's chapel, where King Henry had added the fan-vaulted ceiling with its carved and gilded pendants and blue vault starred with gold. The queen, robed in velvet and fur, lay on a state couch to receive guests. Within another three days the symptoms of puerperal fever became manifest and early on 25 October she died. Her embalmed body, arrayed in gold tissue, the crown upon her head and her hands and breast decked with jewels, lay in state in the palace for nearly three weeks before being taken to Windsor Castle for burial.

Queen Jane's ghost traditionally haunts Hampton Court, like that of her baby son's nurse, Mrs Sibell Penn, and the more clamant spectre of Catherine Howard, King Henry's fifth wife. Legend says that before she left for London and the scaffold in 1542, Queen Catherine tried to appeal to the king, who was at mass. Eluding her guards, she reached the door which leads from Wolsey's gallery to the Holy Day Closet and Royal Pew in the upper part of the chapel, where she was caught and dragged screaming away. For centuries she was supposed to return at night to the door, only to recoil and with ghastly countenance and unearthly cries vanish from sight. So persistent was the story that the scene of her wanderings has long been known as the Haunted Gallery.

The windows in its west wall, opposite the chapel, overlook the Round Kitchen Court, along the north side of which it is continued to Henry VIII's Great Watching Chamber, or Guard Chamber, built in 1535-6. Here the ribs of the richly panelled ceiling curve down to form pendants and the spaces between are filled with bosses displaying the royal arms impaling Seymour, together with the badges of King Henry and Queen Jane. From the Great Watching Chamber, where the Yeomen of the Guard were stationed, their arms ranged upon the walls, visitors passed southward into the chambers of state. The further succession of first-floor rooms continued along the south front of Cloister Green Court, where the king had his private lodging.

Although Wren replaced the royal apartments built by Henry VIII, with the exception of the Great Hall and Great Watching Chamber, major domestic memorials of the king survive. Behind his Great Hall, along the north side, he extended and remodelled Wolsey's culinary empire and today the Great Kitchen is seen to form three connected sections with large open hearths and at either end a serving place. From the serving hatches at the east end attendants carried the dishes up the stairs to the Horn Room, which gave access to the high table, anciently the royal table, on the dais at the east end of the Great Hall. The name Horn Room was conferred in later times, when the apartment became the repository of horns and antlers removed from the walls of the

FACING PAGE: *The Tudor Wine Cellar.*

ABOVE: *Fountain Court which stands on the site of Henry VIII's Cloister Green Court.*

Haunted Gallery, but it was properly a serving annexe for the high table. The other tables were set down the length of the hall, at right angles to the dais, and served by attendants approaching from the serving place at the west end of the Great Kitchen, who carried up the dishes to the Screens Passage under the Minstrels' Gallery at the west end of the hall.

The eastern and central sections of the Great Kitchen appear to be the oldest and may be Wolsey's work. The later western section was probably added by Henry VIII. After Hampton Court Palace ceased to be a royal residence this portion was occupied by a Grace and Favour apartment, until in 1979 it was restored together with its serving place and the door leading further westward into Fish Court, along which King Henry added a string of ancillary kitchens and preparing rooms. The restoration allowed visitors to enjoy a complete view of the Great Kitchen as well as a fascinating glimpse of Fish Court.

Beneath the Great Hall is the King's Beer Cellar, which carries the upper floor on a double row of oak pillars, with sturdy cross-beams. A stone pier in the middle of the cross-wall supports the central hearth of the hall. The Beer Cellar was once a place of continuous activity, as everyone at court, whether noble or simple, man or woman, was allowed a generous daily ration of home-brewed ale, served at "our buttry bar". A maid of honour received a gallon for breakfast, a gallon for dinner, half a gallon in the afternoon and half a gallon at supper. Pitchers of wine were dispensed from the King's New Wine Cellar under the Great Watching Chamber, a brick-vaulted crypt with stone columns and low brick platforms on which the casks rested.

The present Royal Tennis Court at the north-east end of the palace was built about 1625, but King Henry VIII had erected a Close Tennis Court (which still exists, though much disguised) in 1532. He

Continued on page 14

The Verrio Paintings

The paintings on the ceiling of the King's Bedroom (facing page) and the King's Staircase (above) are the work of the celebrated Italian artist Antonio Verrio. For the bedroom he painted an appropriate composition depicting the hunter Endymion lying in the arms of Morpheus, the god of Sleep; above the staircase are gods and goddesses and the heroes of ancient Rome.

Antonio Verrio had worked in his native country and in France before being invited to England by King Charles II, who employed him at Windsor Castle in 1675–1682. His work included wall paintings in St. George's Hall and the former domestic chapel, where he introduced portraits of himself and some of his friends.

Verrio continued to include contemporary portraits when he painted the ceiling of the Great Hall at Chatsworth in 1691 for the Earl (later first Duke) of Devonshire. Here he de-picted the housekeeper, Mrs. Hacket, his enemy of the day, as a witch-like Atropos, one of the Fates who traditionally cut the thread of life. Later, when he was working at Burghley for the 5th Earl of Exeter, he portrayed himself in the Heaven Room, along with Gregory Hascard, Dean of Windsor, to whom he assigned the role of Bacchus, the god of Wine.

For Betty Prick, a pretty housemaid who rejected his amorous advances, he found a place in Hell, where she appeared "with a pack of hell hounds about her". He may have continued the practice at Hampton Court. Walpole, writing to Mann in 1750, told him: "The housekeeper at Windsor, an old monster that Verrio painted as one of the Furies, is dead". This lady was Anne Marriott, daughter of James Marriott, Keeper of the Standing Wardrobe and Privy Lodgings at Hampton Court from 1665–1707.

Anne was living with her parents at Hampton Court when Verrio began painting the King's Staircase about 1700. She was then aged 21. It is tempting to assume that she, like Betty Prick, spurned the passionate Italian and was vengefully portrayed. Although no Furies are depicted in the scenes at Hampton Court, two figures on the King's Staircase may conceivably be identified with Anne Marriott. One is a woman described in Pyne's *Royal Residences* in 1819 as "the genius of Rome, holding a flaming sword, the emblem of destruction, and a bridle, the emblem of government". The other is a nobly proportioned young Atropos at the Banquet of the Gods, where she gazes up at Jove, waiting for his command to cut the thread of human life.

Verrio produced many other murals at Hampton Court from 1700 to 1707 when he died. He is buried nearby.

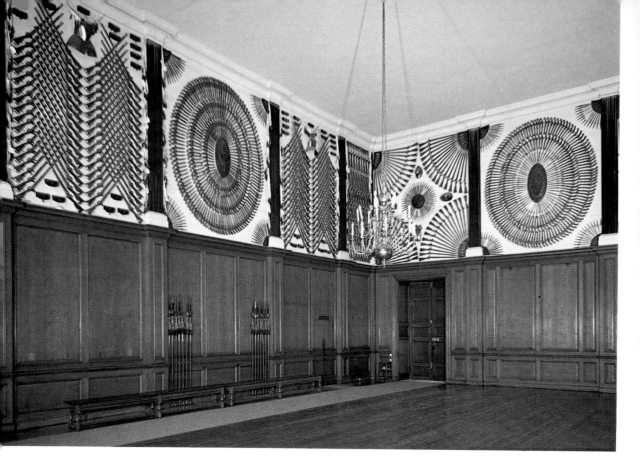

was devoted to the game and to see him playing was said to be "the prettiest thing in the world". According to legend he was engaged in a match at Hampton Court when he received the news that Anne Boleyn's execution had been carried out. At the north-west corner of the grounds he placed the walled and towered Tilt Yard, scene of spectacular tournaments, and on the south, between the palace and the river, created the Pond Garden and the Privy Garden, the former in place of Wolsey's arbours.

Excavation in Clock Court about 1965 revealed foundations of an earlier south range, now outlined in red bricks in the paving: it may have been that of the manor-house of the Knights Hospitallers, demolished when Wolsey built the present picturesque range of "Wolsey Rooms" further south. The astronomical clock from which Clock Court takes its name has a tenuous link with Queen Catherine Howard. It was made for the king by Nicholas Oursian in 1540, the year of her marriage, and placed high on the

inner front of Anne Boleyn's Gate-way, above the first and second storeys and Wolsey's arms. The clock tells the hours, the month, the day of the month, the number of days since the beginning of the year, the phases of the moon and the time of high water at London Bridge.

Although his short-lived queens have left the most abiding memorials, it was King Henry's sixth and last wife, Catherine Parr, who enjoyed the sunniest associations with Hampton Court. They were married there in 1543 and enjoyed many quiet hours together with Prince Edward and his half-sisters, the future Queen Mary I and Queen Elizabeth I. Among the acquisitions with which King Henry enriched his renowned palace were the tapestries which hang today in the Great Hall. They are part of a set representing the *History of Abraham*, woven in Brussels about 1540 by Wilhelm Pannemaker to the designs of Bernard van Orley.

Throughout the history of Hampton Court as a royal residence plays were

presented in the Great Hall. It was the scene of a festive repertoire in 1603, when, after the accession of the House of Stuart, King James I and his consort, Anne of Denmark, spent their first Christmas there The blonde, vivacious queen herself took a leading part in Samuel Daniel's gorgeous masque "The Vision of the Twelve Godesses", which ended the cele-brations. In 1619 she died at Hampton Court, just as the astronomical clock was striking four in the morning. Since that time, it was said, the clock would falter and stop whenever any old resident of the palace passed away.

During the Civil War, King Charles I was held prisoner at Hampton Court

ABOVE: *The King's Guard Chamber. Around its walls hang more than 3000 pieces of armour and weapons arranged by John Harris, Master Gunner of Windsor Castle, who died in 1734.*

FACING PAGE: *The Queen's Gallery. Grinling Gibbons carved the cornice and John Nost the marble chimney-piece in this elegant apartment.*

14

from 24 August 1647 until the following 11 November, when in the dark and stormy evening he escaped through "the room called Paradise" to the river. After his execution Parliament sold most of his possessions and some of the royal palaces, but Hampton Court was retained for the use of the Lord Protector, Oliver Cromwell.

King Charles II filled in the Tudor moat and, on the east side of the palace, laid out the Home Park in its present form. It was he who planted the long avenues of limes radiating from the east front and introduced the great canal. His resources were chiefly directed to Windsor Castle, where he preferred to live, and there was no renaissance of architectural taste at Hampton Court until after his brother, King James II, went into exile. King James's elder daughter, Queen Mary II, and her husband, William Prince of Orange, who ruled as joint sovereigns, formally accepted the crown in the Banqueting House, Whitehall, on 13 February 1689.

King William III, an asthmatic, distrusted the rolling tides and mists which invaded the palace of Whitehall and ten days later he and the queen retired to Hampton Court. By the first of March Sir Christopher Wren had received orders to "beautify and add some new building to that fabric, their Majesties taking great delight in it". Almost immediately he began his work of demolition in Cloister Green Court, which was replaced with the present Fountain Court. Around the quadrangle rose the graceful, many-windowed walls of a palace in the classical style of the period, with cloisters enclosing the lawn and central fountain of the new court.

Wren built his masterpiece in brick beautifully enhanced with Portland stone and designed the interior to provide a superlative setting for sovereignty. In great houses the lord's lodging was usually on the right of the approach from the main gatehouse, and the lady's on the left, and Wren followed tradition by placing the king's suite on the south side of Fountain Court and the queen's on

the north and east. Each had its own Grand Staircase, Guard Chamber, Presence Chamber and Audience Chamber, and beyond these the Drawing Room, which was used as a ceremonial setting for company and in each instance led to the State Bedchamber. In the south-east corner lay the innermost closets where the two state suites joined.

To this point none were accorded the entrée except privileged friends and immediate attendants. For use on state occasions Wren provided the Communication Gallery on the west side of Fountain Court. It leads from the King's Second Presence Chamber to the head of the Queen's Staircase at the north-west corner. Along the south side of the court he placed the Cartoon Gallery in which to display the seven Raphael Cartoons bought by King Charles I in 1623. Today there hangs in the gallery a set of tapestries copied from the cartoons, which Baron Emile d'Erlanger presented to the Crown in 1905. The originals have been at the Victoria and Albert

Museum in London since 1865, when Queen Victoria placed them there on loan, in accordance with the wish of her dead husband, Albert Prince Consort.

In addition to the State Apartments designed for King William and Queen Mary, Wren provided both with private lodgings into which they could retire and relax. The king's private apartments, partly opened to the public in 1978, lay on the ground floor overlooking the Privy Garden on the south and the Fountain Garden to the east. Reached from the Writing Closet above by a small private staircase, they seem to have included two drawing rooms, a dining room, bedchamber and several closets. Three of the closets are now furnished in a style which shows what they may have looked like in King William's time, while a contemporary domestic scene is evoked in the delightful little

Chocolate Kitchen across Chocolate Court. Hot chocolate was a fashionable beverage at the period and enjoyed by King William and his successors.

Base and Clock Courts remained unaltered, except for the addition of the Ionic colonnade on the south side of the latter, which Wren built as an approach to the King's Staircase. It partly masks the Wolsey Rooms.

As early as 16 July 1689 John Evelyn recorded that "a great apartment and spacious gardens with fountains was beginning in the Park at the head of the canal". This was the Great Fountain Garden on the east, which presents so delectable a view from the windows of the Queen's Drawing Room. A vast semicircle of lawn and flowers laid out around the Great Fountain, it has the canal curving around its outer edge and, on the inner side, the Broad Walk separating it from the east front of the palace.

The three windows of the Queen's Drawing Room form part of a centre-piece faced in Portland stone. They are flanked by four Corinthian columns carrying a pediment carved with the figure of Hercules triumphing over Envy, and above the middle window are the initials of William and Mary, with trumpets, drapery, sceptres and a crown. Below the windows three doorways, each closed with a screen

Continued on page 18

*   *   *

ABOVE: *The Communication Gallery, hung with Sir Peter Lely's "Beauties".*

FACING PAGE (above): *William III's State Bedchamber. The bed, chairs and stools were made for the king.* (Below): *The King's First Presence Chamber.*

of delicate wrought iron, lead from the Broad Walk into Fountain Court.

While the work progressed, and especially during her husband's absence on the Irish campaign, Queen Mary made her home in the Water Gallery, a Tudor pavilion on the river bank commonly used as a landing-place for the royal barges. It was converted into a residence for her, "the pleasantest little thing within doors that could possibly be made", and there she was very happy. Like Cardinal Wolsey, she and the king favoured cleanliness, and so there was installed for her a "Bathing Closett", with a white marble bath. She had as a plaything a model dairy with tiles and fitments of finest blue and white delft, the gift of her husband. For the Water Gallery Sir Godfrey Kneller painted the "Hampton Court Beauties", a collection of portraits of her ladies. It makes a companion series to the "Windsor Beauties", Sir Peter Lely's

portraits of the ladies of King Charles II's court, once a focus of admiration at Windsor Castle. These now adorn the walls of the Communication Gallery at Hampton Court.

Although the pretty closet at the corner of the east and south fronts is called Queen Mary's Closet, she never used it. Her apartments were unfinished when on 28 December 1694 she died of smallpox at Kensington Palace. "Upon the death of that illustrious Princess, gardening and all other pleasures were under an eclipse . . . and the beloved Hampton Court lay for some time unregarded." The destruction of Whitehall by fire on 4 January 1698 led King William to resume work there. Soon after 1700 Antonio Verrio was at Hampton Court painting the King's Staircase with its glorious concourse of gods and goddesses and heroes of ancient Rome. The wrought-iron balustrade was the work of Jean Tijou, the French

smith who had come to England with Queen Mary in 1689. Verrio also painted the ceilings of the King's State Bedchamber and Little Bedchamber, the former with Endymion asleep in the arms of Morpheus, the latter with Mars in the lap of Venus. Grinling Gibbons was meanwhile busy in the King's First Presence Chamber, where he carved the oak door cases, the cornice and the festoons of fruit and flowers in limewood. From his hand too came the wonderful overmantel of the white marble fireplace in the King's Drawing Room.

Wren's original plan for rebuilding the entire palace envisaged a grand approach from the north. When the Chestnut Avenue was laid out in Bushy Park by Henry Wise and William Talman in 1699 Wren's idea had already been abandoned, but the alignment of the avenue reflects the vision he had in mind. The piers of the Lion Gate opposite, leading from the

road into the Wilderness, date from Queen Anne's reign and the gates themselves from King George I's. The famous Maze, immediately within the Lion Gate, was planted in Queen Anne's time and is the only surviving feature of the early Wilderness, where artifice produced an effect at variance with the name. Further east the Flower-Pot Gates lead into the Broad Walk, which stretches southward past the east front of the palace to the river, a distance of nearly half a mile. These gates were erected in King William's reign and his initials, together with a crossed sword and sceptre surmounted by a crown, are carved on the Portland stone piers. The Trophy Gates which on the west front open into Outer Green Court and the Great Gatehouse were built for him in 1701 and commemorate his campaigns. The inner pair of red-brick piers carry the "imperiall supporters the Lyon and Unicorn in

Hard Metall . . . and two imperiall shields", cast by the royal master-mason, John Oliver, and erected in June 1701, while the outer pair are surmounted by trophies of arms. Although erected for King William, the "imperiall shields" display the royal arms as borne by the House of Hanover from the accession of King George I until 1801.

The Water Gallery was taken down in 1700 and replaced by the Banqueting House, a miniature palace in plum-coloured brick which Wren almost certainly designed. It has three rooms, the Ante-Room, the Banqueting or Painted Room overlooking the river, and the Closet or withdrawing-room. Verrio painted the ceiling and wall-panels in the Banqueting Room and Gibbons carved the frames of the mirrors between the windows.

That same year the Privy Garden was laid out anew by Talman and Wise. The Orangery, 157 feet long, at that

time held orange trees which on summer days stood out on the terrace opposite the garden. Queen Anne, after her accession in 1702, added the Lower Orangery along the south front of Base Court.

It was Queen Anne who first occupied the rooms planned for her dead sister. Verrio returned in 1702 to paint several apartments for her, including the Queen's Drawing Room, and stayed until five years later he died

*　　*　　*

FACING PAGE: *The Queen's Drawing Room. On the south wall is Verrio's painting of the British Fleet at anchor.*

ABOVE: *One of the twelve panels of the wrought-iron screen made by Jean Tijou for the gardens of Hampton Court.*

themselves, and their son Frederick, later Prince of Wales.

Following the accession of King George II the Prince of Wales's Suite at the north-east corner of the palace, designed for him by Sir John Vanbrugh, was used by his son and daughter-in-law, Princess Augusta, the parents of King George III. It was from these rooms that the imprudent Frederick, to annoy his parents, hurried his young wife in a coach to London when she was about to give birth to her first child. They are connected with the cloister of Fountain Court by a pretty balconied staircase, on the walls of which now hang three pieces of Mortlake tapestry illustrating the battle of the English and Dutch fleets off Solebay in 1672.

Additional state rooms were completed by King George II in 1732. The date is carved over the George II Gateway, which leads from Clock Court into Fountain Court. In the range above is the handsome Cumberland Suite, probably built to the designs of William Kent and occupied for a time by the king's soldier-son, William Augustus, Duke of Cumberland. As George II on occasion followed the ancient royal custom of dining in public, a charming music room on the east front, originally fitted up in 1715-18, was adapted for the purpose. It is still called the King's Public Dining Room, but retains its early Georgian panelling, painted turquoise with a gilded cornice, and the striking marble fireplace attributed to Gibbons.

In 1735 Kent painted the walls and ceiling of the Queen's Staircase, which

Continued on page 22

*   *   *

ABOVE: *In the Queen's Presence Chamber, opened in 1978, stands Queen Anne's bed with its matching suite of furniture. It was made for her state bedchamber at Windsor Castle in 1714 and has its original canopy and head, inner and outer valances, curtains, coverlet and lower valances of cerise and lemon cut velvet on a cream satin ground, with a predominant pattern of pots of flowers.*

FACING PAGE: *The ceiling of the Queen's Bedchamber depicts Aurora, the Dawn Goddess, rising from the waves. It was painted by Sir James Thornhill in 1715.*

and was buried at "Hamtonn", probably in the vault under the parish church. The decorations of the Chapel Royal, including the oak reredos carved by Gibbons, were designed by Wren for Queen Anne, in whose reign the Royal Pew was panelled and the ceiling painted by Sir James Thornhill, who also introduced the *trompe l'oeil* window at the south-east end in order to mask a view of domestic buildings.

After her death and the accession of the House of Hanover in 1714, Thornhill was employed by King George I to paint the ceiling of the Queen's Bedroom. The theme is Aurora rising in her chariot from the sea. King George had divorced his wife, Sophia Dorothea of Celle, and the room was used by the Prince and Princess of Wales, later King George II and Queen Caroline. The deep cove has medallion portraits of King George I, the prince and princess

like the King's Staircase has a wrought-iron balustrade by Tijou. A suite of private rooms on the east side of Fountain Court, parallel to the Queen's State Rooms, includes the Queen's Bathing Closet. It was Queen Caroline's and contains a tall marble-lined recess with basin and tap. Most of the rooms are oak-panelled, but one of them, known as the King's Private Chamber, displays a rare example of flock wallpaper dating from the 1730s.

There is a story that in his irascible old age King George II was walking one day in the State Apartments with his grandson, the future King George III. Angered by some remark he turned and boxed the prince's ears. The memory rankled and after his accession in 1760 George III would not live at Hampton Court. Visitors who could afford a fee were admitted to the State Apartments, their payments being granted to the State Housekeeper as part of her emolument. After the death in April 1838 of Lady Emily Montagu the office was abolished and in the following November Queen Victoria opened the State Apartments to the public without charge. People were already free to worship in the Chapel Royal, where services are still held on Sundays and Saints' Days.

Discreet restoration has helped to make Hampton Court the authentic memorial it is today. Although the two upper storeys of the Great Gatehouse were removed in 1770, and much of the facing brickwork renewed about a century later, the effect remains imposing. The heavy Tudor oak doors carved with linenfold panels were replaced in 1882 after serving for years as the floor of a carpenter's workshop. In 1910 the moat was excavated and the bridge, built by King Henry VIII to replace an earlier one, found complete except for its parapet, which was renewed together with the King's Beasts on either side. Along the north front, in Tennis Court Lane, the chimney stacks of the kitchen range preserve the full inventiveness of Tudor design, so careful was the work of the craftsmen who copied the originals.

Continued on page 24

*   *   *

ABOVE: *The Long Water. Beyond the Great Fountain the vista is continued eastward into the Home Park, created by Charles II.*

FACING PAGE (above): *The Banqueting Room, part of William III's detached Banqueting House overlooking the River Thames. The wall panels and ceiling were painted by Verrio. (Below): The Great Vine. Of the Black Hamburgh variety it was planted in the reign of George III.*

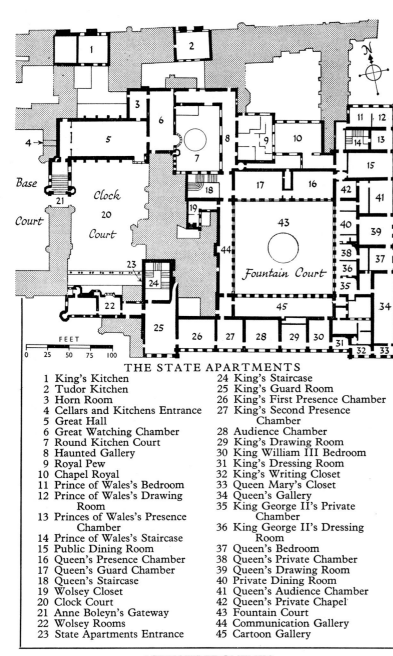

THE STATE APARTMENTS

1 King's Kitchen
2 Tudor Kitchen
3 Horn Room
4 Cellars and Kitchens Entrance
5 Great Hall
6 Great Watching Chamber
7 Round Kitchen Court
8 Haunted Gallery
9 Royal Pew
10 Chapel Royal
11 Prince of Wales's Bedroom
12 Prince of Wales's Drawing Room
13 Princes of Wales's Presence Chamber
14 Prince of Wales's Staircase
15 Public Dining Room
16 Queen's Presence Chamber
17 Queen's Guard Chamber
18 Queen's Staircase
19 Wolsey Closet
20 Clock Court
21 Anne Boleyn's Gateway
22 Wolsey Rooms
23 State Apartments Entrance
24 King's Staircase
25 King's Guard Room
26 King's First Presence Chamber
27 King's Second Presence Chamber
28 Audience Chamber
29 King's Drawing Room
30 King William III Bedroom
31 King's Dressing Room
32 King's Writing Closet
33 Queen Mary's Closet
34 Queen's Gallery
35 King George II's Private Chamber
36 King George II's Dressing Room
37 Queen's Bedroom
38 Queen's Private Chamber
39 Queen's Drawing Room
40 Private Dining Room
41 Queen's Audience Chamber
42 Queen's Private Chapel
43 Fountain Court
44 Communication Gallery
45 Cartoon Gallery

ACKNOWLEDGMENTS

All photographs of the State Apartments, the Chapel Royal, the Great Hall and Wolsey's Closet are reproduced by gracious permission of Her Majesty The Queen and are Crown Copyright reserved. The plan and other photographs in this book, except those mentioned below, are reproduced by permission of the Department of the Environment and are likewise Crown Copyright reserved. The front and back covers are by A. F. Kersting, A.I.I.P., F.R.P.S. All the portraits—except that of Jane Seymour on page ii cover which is in the Kunsthistorisches Museum, Vienna—are from the National Portrait Gallery and are reproduced by courtesy of the Trustees. New information in the book is based on research by Mr H. M. Colvin for The History of the King's Works, Vol. V. We wish also to acknowledge the kind help and advice of Miss Juliet Allan, Inspector of Ancient Monuments, Department of the Environment.

The dial of the astronomical clock, being no longer in working order, was banished to a store-room after the erection in 1835 of the clock on the outer side of Anne Boleyn's Gateway. The latter, made in 1799, came from St. James's Palace. In 1879 new mechanism was made for the astronomical clock and the dial replaced. It has since been repainted in the original colours revealed by cleaning. In the 18th-century campanile above the gateway hang two clock bells, the larger of which was made about 1479. Ernest Law, the dedicated historian of Hampton Court, liked to think that it was one of the bells mentioned in the schedule of Wolsey's lease of the manor.

From the cardinal's time to that of King George II gilded state barges were a familiar sight on the river front. The graceful picture, often rendered still more agreeable by a band of music, is commemorated in the name Barge Walk given to the riverside path bounding the gardens. Between Barge Walk and the Privy Garden stands the magnificent Tijou Screen of twelve wrought-iron panels, or gates, 10 feet 6 inches high, which Tijou made originally for the Great Fountain Garden.

Although King George III deserted Hampton Court he did not neglect it. The Great Vine of the Black Hamburgh variety, which originated in a slip from the one at Valentine's at Ilford in Essex, was planted in 1768 in a corner of the Pond Garden. The path to the Vinery passes the Knot Garden at the angle where Wren's south front joins the Tudor range. It was created in 1924 in the style fashionable in the reign of Queen Elizabeth I, whose initials, ER, together with the date 1568, appear on the stonework of the bay window above. To the left, between the Knot Garden and the octagonal angle turret which still bears its original lead cupola, are the windows of the Wolsey Rooms.

Also in 1924 the Tilt Yard was laid out with lawns and a rose-garden and the Tudor tower, sole survivor of five which once overlooked it, made into a teahouse. The rest had been removed in King William III's reign, when the Tilt Yard became a kitchen garden. Today it is a matured and peaceful resort, where a restaurant and cafeteria by no means detract from the monumental grandeur of Hampton Court.

SBN 85372 056 8